This book belongs to...

_____

BLOOMSBURY
Activity Books

First published 2013 by Bloomsbury Publishing Plc
50 Bedford Square, London, WC1B 3DP

www.bloomsbury.com

Text copyright © 2013 Bloomsbury Publishing Plc
Illustrations copyright © 2013 Katy Jackson & Nellie Ryan

ISBN 978-1-4081-8222-2

A CIP record for this book is available from the British Library.
All rights reserved. No part of this book may be reproduced or transmitted
in any form or by any means, electronic or mechanical, including photocopying,
recording, or by any information storage and retrieval system,
without permission in writing from the publisher.

This book is produced using paper that is made from wood grown in
managed, sustainable forests. It is natural, renewable and recyclable.
The logging and manufacturing processes conform to the
environmental regulations of the country of origin.

Printed in China by Leo Paper Products.

1 3 5 7 9 10 8 6 4 2

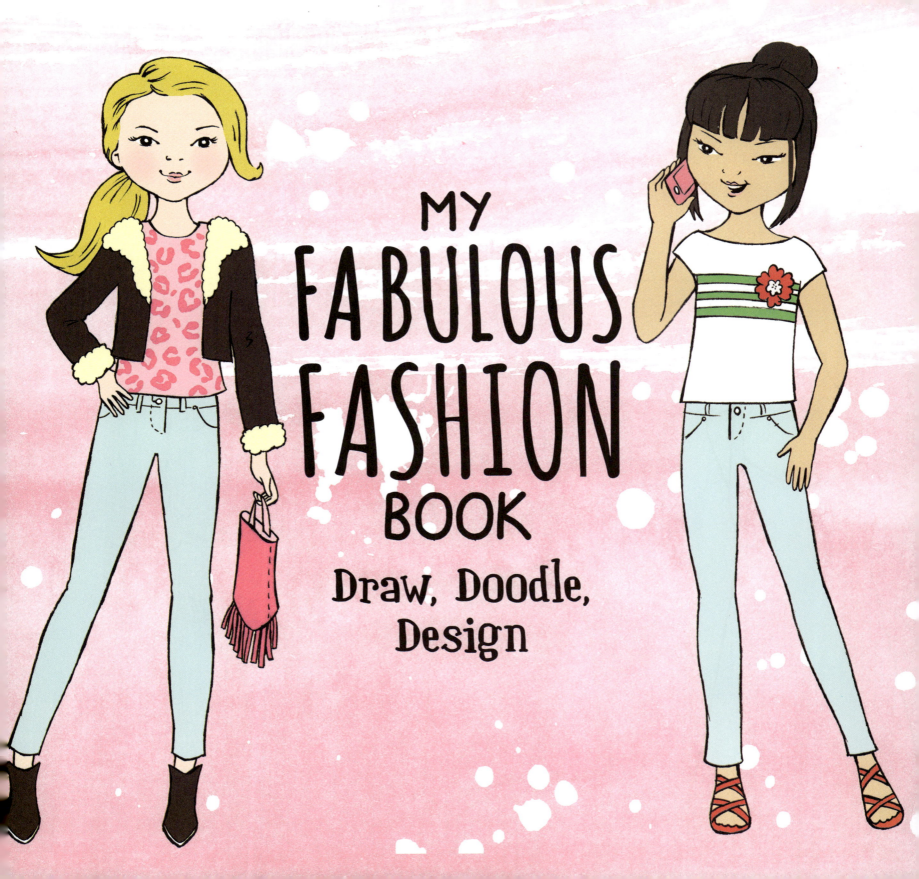

DRESS TO IMPRESS

A designer is putting together her latest collection. Can you help her finish off her dresses?

JEAN ART

Help Laura, Tina, Mia and Farah customise their jeans with jewels, patches, embroidery and more! Use the ideas on the page and stickers to help you.

LAURA

ALL DRESSED UP!

Finish off these patterns and colour these beautiful dresses so they are ready for the shop window.

BRIGHT BOWS

Everything looks brighter with a bow! Finish and decorate these items using bow doodles and stickers.

FLORAL FANCIES

Floral patterns are fresh and pretty. Add some to these clothes. Use the ideas below to help you.

BIRDS AND BUTTERFLIES

Add pretty birds and butterflies to these clothes. Use the stickers to help you.

BEADS

Design and colour in your own bead necklaces. Use the stickers to help you.

SALON STYLE
Help this hairdresser out by giving these girls gorgeous new hairdos.

FABULOUS EARRINGS

Finish off and add more pairs of earrings to Tina's jewellery stand. Which ones will she pick to wear with her outfit?

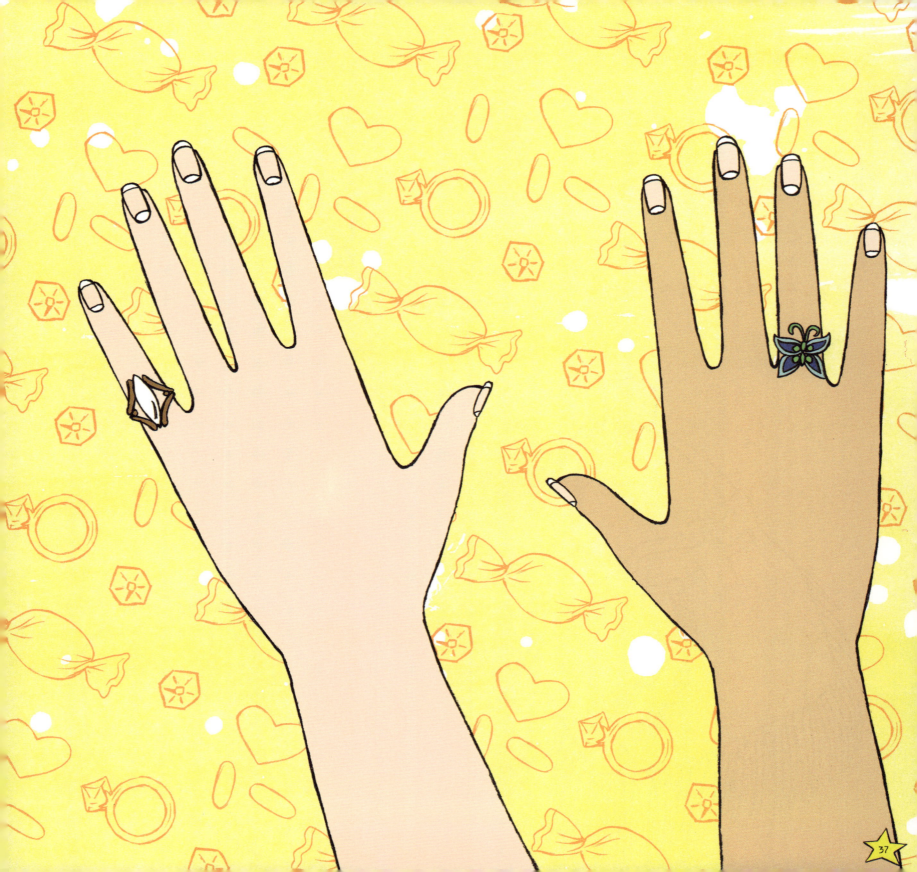

HANDBAGS

Design and decorate these handbags. Use the stickers to help you.

ACCESSORIZE ME!

These girls are twins. Add accessories to complete their looks. Use the ideas on the page to help you.

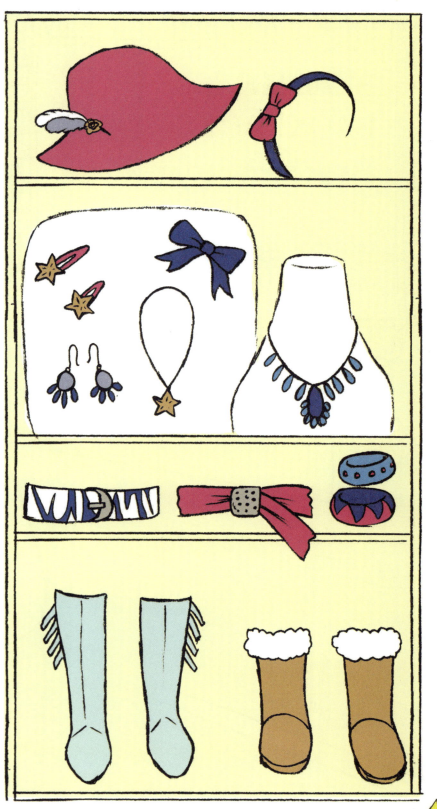

SENSATIONAL SUNGLASSES

Design some great sunglasses to help the girls stay cool in the sun.

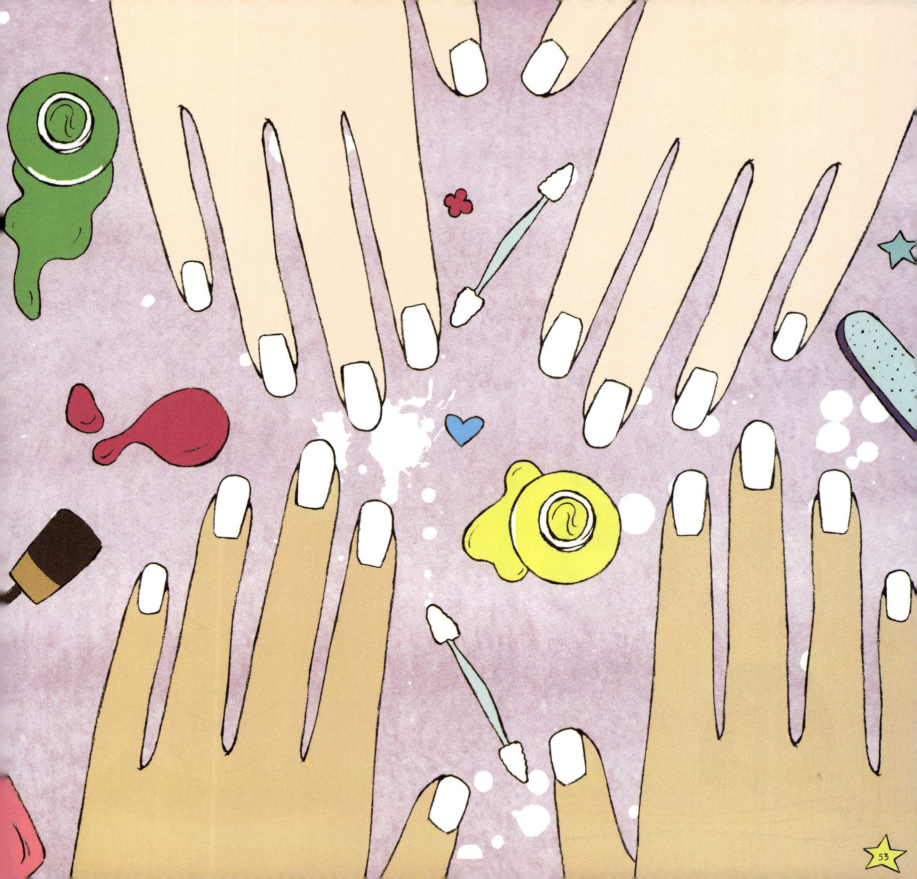

FABULOUS HAIR

Give these girls hairstyles to match their looks. Use the ideas below to help you.

NEW LOOK

Mia would like to try out some new looks. Draw two new hairstyles for her. Use the ideas below to help you.

BRILLIANT BANGLES

Design some brilliant bangles here.

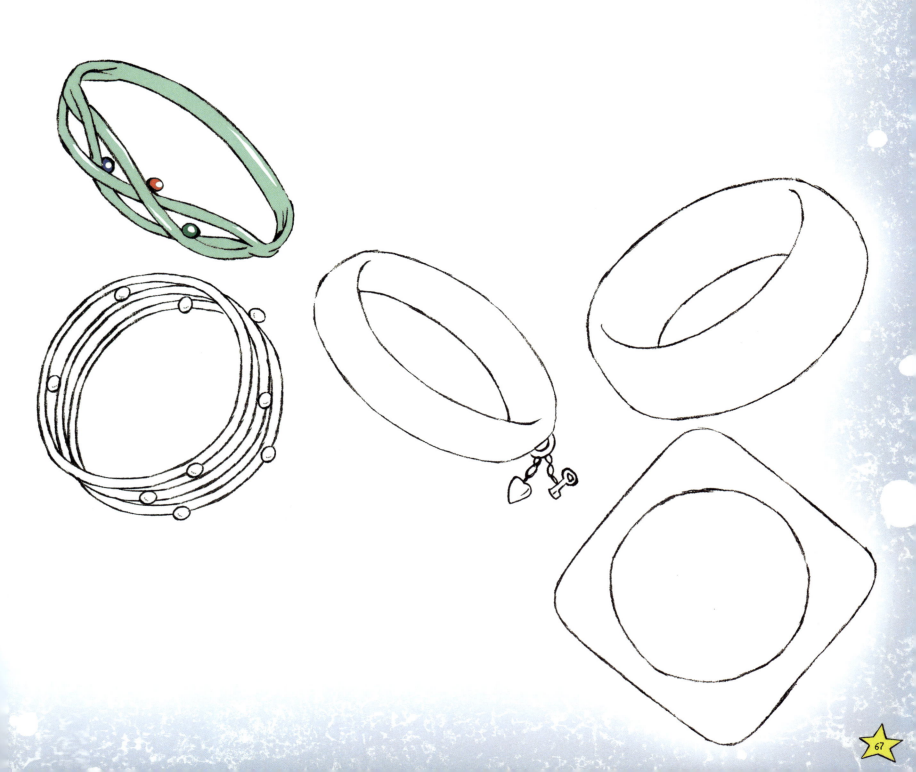

HOLLYWOOD HAIR

Create some showstopping hairstyles for these stars. Use the ideas below to help you.

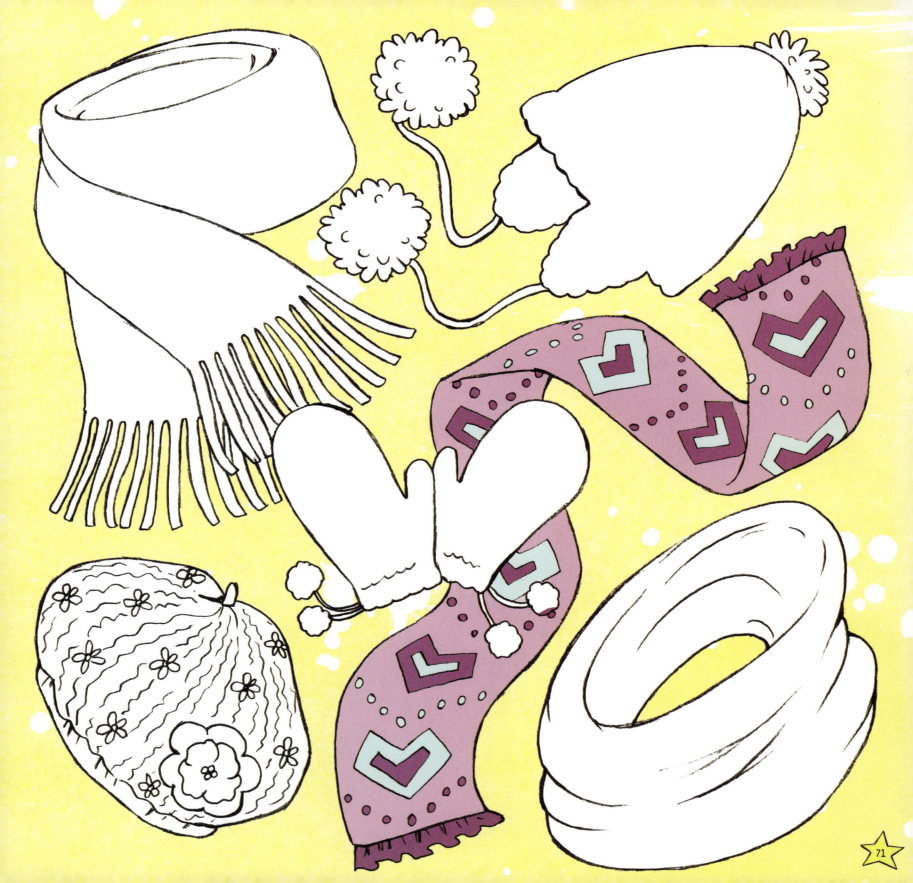

PERFECT PRINCESSES

Help the princesses find the perfect tea dresses to attend the Palace Garden Party.

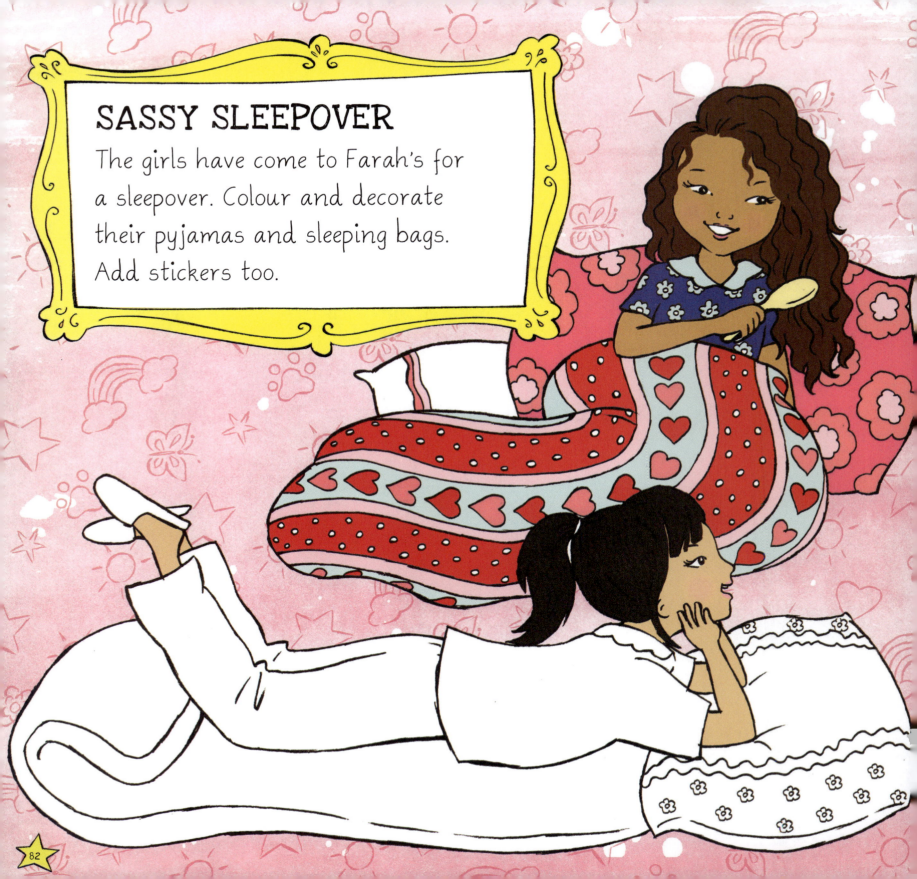

Design and draw your dream outfit in the space below.